THE SKILL ARTIST'S GUIDE TO CHESS

CONQUER YOUR FRIENDS WITH 8 EASY PRINCIPLES

Table of Contents

CHAPTER 1: IMPROVE YOUR CHESS GAME FASTER...THE SKILL ARTIST WAY

My name is Maxen Tarafa, and I'm a Skill Artist. No, I'm not going to ask you to find a walnut under a cup or join a pyramid scheme. I want to show you how you can play Chess at an intermediate level in an alarmingly short amount of time.

If you're anything like me, you want to play a good or *very good* game of Chess, but you're not interested in becoming the next Garry Kasparov. You just want to know a few moves and maybe **conquer all your friends!** Enter the art of learning new skills. Or, what I call Skill Art.

My approach is simple. In most any skill, if you learn and apply five to ten of the most critical lessons, you'll be at least twice as good as the beginner. However, most books written by experts are either going to be an A to Z instruction book or they're going to be designed for the in-crowd.

Let me be the first to say, I'm not an expert in Chess. I'm a guy who learns skills in a short amount of time, and I want to give you an extended cheat sheet that can help you do what I did, but faster.

I guarantee there's going to be a lot of "Chess experts" who don't like this. I'm ready for the hate mail. After all, Chess is supposed to be hard and complicated and cold and logical and emotionless, right? But I'm confident that if you read this book and practice the 8 principles I provide, not only will you have a great time reading it, you will also have a significant edge over your opponents.

How am I so confident they'll work? First, they worked for me. In college, my roommate and I played Chess regularly. Neither of us was trained, but we enjoyed playing. After I graduated from college, I wanted to get better and I dedicated myself to playing Chess for at least 3 hours a day for about 3 months. When I started out my rating started in the low 600s.

I'd been playing Chess for more than 10 years and I was only in the 600s! (Just a point of reference, master level is 2200 and up). After studying everything I could find on the internet and practicing, I more than doubled my rating up to 1300! These eight principles still stand out to me as the most important.

Second, I taught these principles to people I know. When my brother was 9 years old, the only thing he knew was how to move the pieces. I taught him these 8 principles and a week later he was beating 16 and 17 year olds.

There is one principle in particular that I taught to an exceptionally talented student named Eduardo when I was a Chess coach at my friend's high school. He applied one principle and it *changed his game completely*. None of us could beat him after that–including me!

When I was preparing to write this book, I told my friend Gus, who trained competitively as a kid, that I was writing a guide for beginners about eight principles that will greatly impact their game. He said, "Oh yeah, you can totally tell a difference between trained players and people who have never studied Chess." He then went on to list four of the eight techniques I was already planning to use!

Before I started practicing Chess, I thought only "logical" people could be good at Chess. As a writing and arts oriented person, I never thought I could be competitive with my more "logical" friends. What I realized after training myself is that no matter who you are, you can learn ANYTHING. If you can read, practice, and use a computer you can learn these techniques in a week!

I won't mention any names. But some of my longtime friends and family who used to destroy me when I was young can't beat me anymore. One of my friends actually said to me, "Dude, I haven't beaten you since you started playing on the Internet." What I didn't tell him was that I wasn't just playing. I was training.

All in all, these are some of the nastiest and most effective techniques for post-beginners and they are sure to help you conquer your friends. Just remember, with great power comes great responsibility.

Sincerely,

Maxen R. Tarafa

www.theskillartistsguide.com

CHAPTER 2: HOW TO LEARN FROM THIS BOOK

Unlike most Chess books, in this book you'll find no complex Chess notation. You also won't find lengthy discussions of the games of Chess Masters. There are only principles, simple (if crude) illustrations of those principles, and links to videos or external website to help you understand the principle.

I'm assuming a few things in the title of this book. First, I'm assuming your friends aren't formally trained Chess players. If they are, and you want to beat them, this book can give you a big leg up. Second, I'm assuming that you already know the basics of Chess. I created this book for casual Chess players who have played for years but never studied the game. If you're an absolute beginner you can still use this book, but you might want to review the basics.

Here's a great Youtube playlist by Howcast that will show you the basics of Chess:

How to Set up the Board [continue the playlist for how to Move the Pieces]
http://youtu.be/wH9Z1ORrtjQ?list=PLLALQuK1NDriznzxP5rQkQwKIrGSWRMZF

Legal & Illegal Moves | Chess
http://youtu.be/ZeEEurdg0tE?list=PLLALQuK1NDriznzxP5rQkQwKIrGSWRMZF

How to Move the King [and checkmate]
http://youtu.be/1xz3588Qumo?list=PLLALQuK1NDriznzxP5rQkQwKIrGSWRMZF

When creating this book, I designed each chapter to be as short and easy to remember as possible. Of course, there's more to learn, but that will come later. The important thing is that you learn and remember the principle and then practice.

I would suggest that before you start learning the 8 principles that you go to Chess.com (You'll see a lot references to Chess.com. I swear they're not a sponsor, I just really like the website). Sign up for a free account and play Live Chess. Live Chess is cool because you can play people from across the world and even chat with them if you'd like. But the point is to get yourself a rating.

I know you mainly just want to stomp on *your* friends via Chess. But the reason I say to get a rating is that you can easily accelerate your learning when you can set measurable goals and work to obtain them. If you never know where you're starting, you'll never know how far you've come, or how far you *want* to go.

A note on the links and videos, I use a lot of them. If your device is connected to the Internet, you can just click on the link and a browser window should open. If it's not connected to the Internet, I provided the title of the video so you can easily just search it in Youtube with your computer.

Author's Note: If you bought the softcover version, and you don't want to search or type every video or link, go to my website theskillartistsguide.com/chess-resources where you will find all the links organized by chapter on one page. You can also get the Kindle version for free from Amazon. You're welcome!

You don't have to watch every single video, but if you want to get a better idea of the principle, check it out. I realize Youtube videos probably aren't the most academically sound way to teach. But luckily, I don't care! As a skill artist, I look for clear, quality information, and if it can help me learn quickly, I use it!

As you read, you may want to play with a Chessboard next to you. Or with a Chess Program (such as Chess.com) open in a separate window. It will help to practice the principles as you go (especially if you're a kinesthetic learner).

The principles are listed in order of what you are most likely to encounter. After you've read the book, and you're ready to practice, re-read the principles you want to practice. Then, apply them, keeping them in mind as you play.

Alright, let's get to the good stuff. Here are 8 principles that will help you conquer your friends in Chess.

CHAPTER 3: 8 PRINCIPLES THAT WILL HELP YOU CONQUER YOUR FRIENDS

PRINCIPLE #1: CONTROL THE CENTER

You know how I can tell a Chess Player from a Monopoly player? It's their first move. Most novices will choose a piece they think is the most interesting. Some choose a piece they think is safe. Those are both fine as long as you also do one thing...**Control the Center.** Whoever controls the center controls the game.

What do I mean by the center? **In the picture below**, I've highlighted the four squares that make up the center. Think of these as your **Power Squares.**

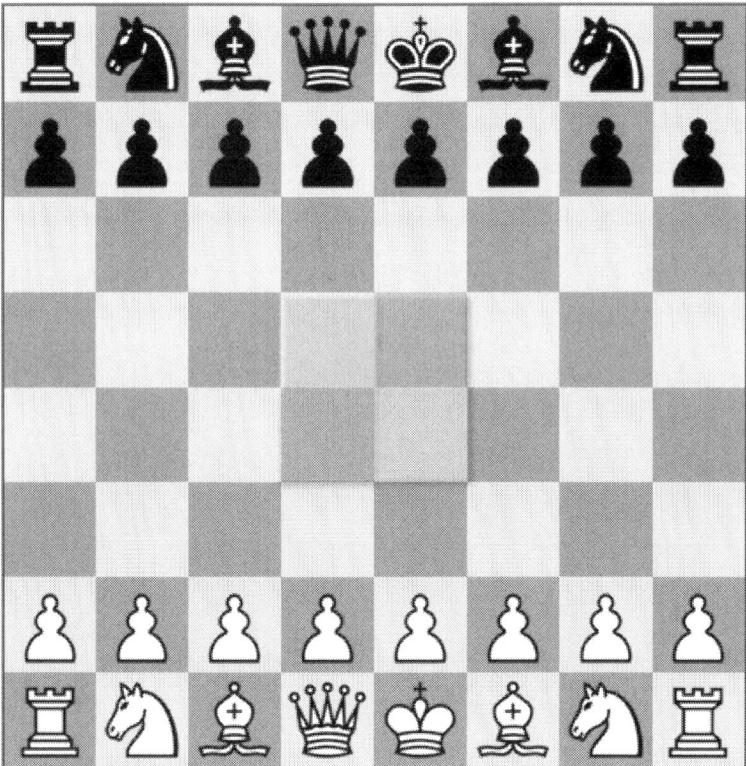

In the beginning of the game, every move you make should fight to control those four squares. That means most likely your first move will be one of those center Pawns followed by your Knights and your Bishops. **In the picture below**, I show what your pieces would look like if they were developed to control those four squares.

The Best Defense is a Good Offense

It goes without saying that you want to attack your enemy before he attacks you. If you're only playing defense, he'll eventually break you down and you're going to lose.

Notice that each of the middle squares is poised for attack by at least one (sometimes two) of white's pieces. This development shows the best control of the center. Of course, this arrangement is nearly impossible in a real game. But when you're choosing an opening or creating an opening for yourself, keep in mind that any decent opening will use a variation of this set-up.

Why is it so important to control the center?

Let me put it this way. Controlling the Center is like controlling the stereo when you're with your jerkhole older brother on a road trip. If you connect *your* iPhone first, you can choose from a variety of your favorite musicians. If your jerkhole older brother connects his, you can only choose among Justin Bieber, NIckelback, and Chumbawumba and you're going to have to choose among *his* favorite bands. Which would you rather have?

Center control is closely related to development. If you control the center, it makes it very hard for your opponent to develop his pieces (or bad taste in music) past the center or move his good pieces toward your King. The center is the fastest and easiest place to damage your opponent from. So, the person who controls it has far more opportunities to attack.

What this means is: You want to move your central Pawns, Knights, and Bishops first. You want to move your Rooks and the six side Pawns last.

Controlling the center requires a good opening. There are literally hundreds of openings to choose from, but I guarantee they all try to **Control the Center.**

PRINCIPLE #2: TRADE ALL THE WAY DOWN

This one's a two-parter that will increase your offensive power tenfold.

Part 1: **Know the Piece Values.** Many beginning players don't know exactly what each piece is worth. Most people know that Pawns are the least valuable, but you need to know the exact point value of each piece in a pinch. Here's a breakdown:

Piece	Image	Value	Explanation
King		Ultimate	The **King** is infinitely valuable. If you checkmate the King, the game's over.
Queen		9 pts.	The **Queen** is the most powerful piece on the board and the next most valuable after the King. Only trade your Queen for another Queen, two rooks, or a Checkmate.

Rook		5 pts.	The **Rook** is the next most valuable because of how much space it can cover. It's especially strong in the endgame.
Bishop		3 pts.	The **Bishop** is a great piece that can stretch across the board.
Knight		3 pts.	The **Knight** is my personal favorite. Technically, it's equal in value as the Bishop, but the Knight is tricky and can win you free pieces.
Pawn		1 pt.	The **Pawns** are the workhorse of your Chess army. You can trade a Pawn for any other piece, and don't be shy about trading it for position early in the game. In the endgame, however, the Pawn's value skyrockets (more on this later).

WHY YOU WANT TO KNOW THE VALUE OF EACH PIECE

In Chess, you can't simply keep all your pieces safe and sound til the end of the game. Luckily, it's not like the first Harry Potter where Ron will die if he's taken by another piece. If you want to win, you're going to have to trade. And to make good trades, you have to know what each piece is worth.

How is the value of the piece going to influence your trading?

First, when you're considering a trade, it's not always as simple as a Bishop for a Bishop. Sometimes you actually have to do the math when trading, say, a Queen for two Rooks.

Second, even when you're considering an equal trade. It's good to know how many total points each opponent owns. If your opponent owns more total points, you want to avoid equal trades. Personally, I like trades where my opponent loses points (cue nefarious pipe organ music).

PART 2: TRADE ALL THE WAY DOWN

Once you have more points than your opponent, you can make equal trades all day. I see a lot of beginners try to conserve their pieces. Don't do this! If your opponent accidentally sacrifices her Knight, Bishop, Rook, or Queen, you now have a significant edge in points. Now you can **Trade All the Way Down.**

What is Trading All the Way Down? Let's say your opponent accidentally gives you her Rook. That's worth 5 points! If you trade your second Rook for her second Rook, your Bishop for her Bishop, your Bishop for her Knight, your Knight for her Bishop, your Queen for her Queen, and so on. You're still ahead by a *whole Rook!*

That's Trading All the Way Down: When you're ahead, make equal trades until most the pieces are gone from the board and you're still ahead by one piece. Now, she has fewer pieces to protect her King. The game will shortly end in your favor.

Moral of the story, don't try to save every single piece. That's just more risk that you will make a mistake and lose your edge. Once you're ahead, **Trade All the Way Down.**

If you went to war tomorrow, would you rather have a tank or a pistol? These are your weapons of attack. And they can be harder to learn. But if you learn how to use them and you start looking for them in your Chess games, you will conquer.

In the example above, I mentioned that if your friend *accidentally* gives you his Rook then you can **Trade All the Way Down**. What if you could *take* his Rook and not lose a piece of your own? Well, you could still **Trade All the Way Down**.

That's what **Forks, Pins, and Skewers** achieve. When executed correctly, they give you a *huge* lead for nothing. Let's talk about Forks first since they're my favorite.

A **Fork** is when a Knight, Bishop, Rook, or Queen attacks two pieces on different squares at the same time. In the **image below**, a Knight has forked a Queen and a Rook. Notice the "fork" shape the arrows make.

The opponent can move either the Queen or the Rook, but he can't move both! You'll notice that the Queen and Rook are protecting each other, but it doesn't matter. You remember that the value of a Queen is 9 points and a Rook is 5 while a Knight is only 3 points. So, White will gladly make that trade any day.

While my favorite piece to fork with is the Knight. You can also fork with Bishops, Rooks, and Queens. Here are a few examples.

19

A Bishop Forks two Rooks.

A Rook forks a Knight and Bishop.

A Knight forking a Queen and Rook.

In the **picture above**, notice that the King can't take the White Knight because the Bishop protects it. From the beginning of the game, I am trying to put my Knight in this position. The game is in my favor from here on out.

PINS

A **Pin** is when your piece traps (or pins) your opponent's piece between it and the opponent's King. In the example below, Black's Rook would love to move down and eat up the White Queen, but it can't because moving down would put the King in Check, which is illegal. The Rook is pinned. Since two pieces are attacking that square, White's Queen can move up and take the Rook. Since the Black King can't attack back, White takes a free piece. Oh yeah!

A **Skewer** is when your piece attacks two opponent pieces through each other. **See the image below**. The difference between a skewer and a pin is that the Queen in this situation is not pinned to the Rook. It *can* move and if your opponent is smart, he *will* move it. But one of those pieces is going to die. It's called a Skewer because it's like a shish-kebab that skewers through two pieces of grilled chicken.

Bishop skewers Black King and Rook

A **Discovered Check** is not technically a Fork, Pin, or Skewer, but it's in the same family of awesome moves and I wanted to share it with you because it's just as powerful. I also call it the **Peekaboo Maneuver**. Discovered Check is when a piece that could attack the opponent's King is blocked by one of your own pieces. When you move the blocking piece out of the way, your opponent **discovers** he's in check. In the **picture below**, the White Rook is pointed toward the Black King, but White's own bishop blocks it.

Rook is pointed toward Black's King, but is intentionally blocked by his own Bishop.

Peekaboo! White takes advantage of Discovered Check,
attacking the Queen while the King must move out of check.

In the next picture, White's Bishop is moved out of the way. Notice that the Rook is putting the King into check and the Bishop is attacking Black's Queen. Since the King must move out of check immediately, White's Bishop can take Black's Queen for free. Booyah.

If you want to pull ahead in points, **Forks, Pins, and Skewers**, and **Discovered Check** are the best way to do it. In order to incorporate them into your repertoire you'll have to actively look for opportunities to use them. But I promise, once you got it, it's like bringing a laser gun to a knife fight.

Did you know there are three *special* moves in Chess? Most novices don't know about them. In fact, if you do one of them, most novices will think you're cheating and you will have to prove to them they're real. One of those moves is **Castling** and it's one of the most important moves you can do.

---

3 Special Moves

There are 3 special moves in Chess: *Castling, En Passant, and Promoting.* In this book, we'll cover Castling and Promoting.

Castling is when, after you have **cleared the pieces between a King and a Rook**, and you have moved **neither the King nor the Rook**. You can move the **King two spaces** toward your Rook of choice, and move the **Rook to the other side of the King** in a single turn.

What!?

Yeah. It's real. Here's a Youtube video of a very sophisticated man showing you how to castle:

Beginning Chess Lessons: Part 2 : What is Castling in a Chess Game
https://www.youtube.com/watch?v=nECzHBY6sEY

A King and Rook just before Castling.

A King and a Rook right after Castling

When I first used this move on my nine-year-old brother, he started to cry and exclaimed that I was cheating. That's how powerful this move is. Remember, with great power comes great responsibility.

So, why is this move one of the most important things you can learn? Here's why:

1. It blows people's minds
2. It moves your King out of the center where he is protected by Pawns
3. It releases your Rook to wreak havoc on your opponent
4. It allows you to dodge your opponent's attack

Have you ever seen a football game where a running back with the ball jukes a defender and runs ten more yards? That's what this is. It's a juke for your King. At least, that's how I thought of it before I got good.

Before I dedicated myself to getting better at Chess, I knew what Castling was, I just didn't know how or when to use it. You're going to learn right now what took me years to figure out: **Castle Early, Castle Often**

Before I knew how to Castle, I would wait until the moment my opponent was just about to launch an attack on my King. And then castled.

 It sounds like a good idea, but the problem is by the time your opponent is close enough to your King to attack, he may be able to prevent you from castling. Remember that your King can't be in check, cannot pass through check, and cannot pass into check when castling. If you wait until the final moment, it may be too late. In other words, **the best time to Castle is as soon as possible. Castle Early, Castle Often.**

Instead of thinking of Castling as a defensive move, think of it as an offensive move. Castling opens your Rook to contribute to your offense. Instead of your Rook sitting in the corner until the end of the game, it's now able to protect your other pieces, and/or attack the other side of the board.

 If we're thinking about it from a points perspective, you have 5 more attacking points at the *beginning* of the game. That's huge. If the god of Chess floated down from the sky and said to you, "take this powerful extra piece that you can use in the beginning of the game," and handed you a Rook, you'd take it.

Now, you can still use it as juke for your King if you have to, but if you want to utterly destroy your friends in Chess…**Castle Early, Castle Often.**

PRINCIPLE #5: KEEP YOUR QUEEN BACK

Many novices know about this. It's one of the first things you learn when you formally take on Chess, but I'm including it here because it's one of the most important things you will *ever* learn in Chess….and possibly in life. **Do not move your Queen!**

Okay, you remember that, right? Good. Now I'm going to modify that statement. **Do not move your Queen…*until your other pieces are developed.* Keep your Queen Back.** You knew it was coming because you've moved your Queen before and the Chess police didn't come to arrest you. But when you move beyond the beginner level of Chess, you'll want to keep your Queen back. The reason you want to keep your Queen back is:

1. Your Queen protects your King
2. Your Queen protects your center Pawns (which control the center. See principle #1)
3. Your Queen is your most powerful piece (if you lose it at the beginning, you're screwed)
4. If you move your Queen too early, you lose critical time to develop your other pieces

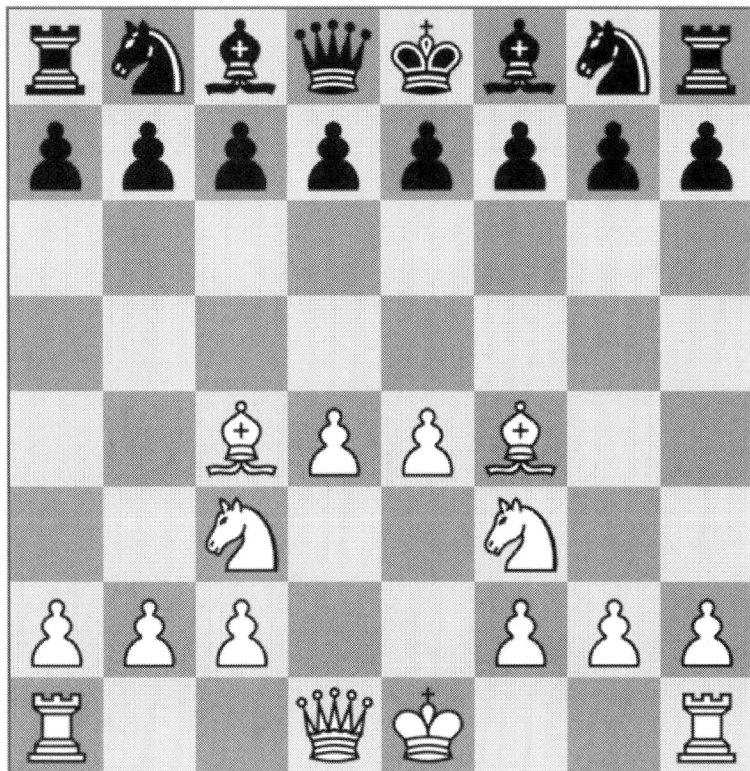

The picture above shows all of the pieces after they're developed. After your pieces are developed is a good time to move your Queen.

Reason number 4 is the most important. Let me tell you a little story about a kid named Eduardo.

EDUARDO

Once upon a time, I had a friend who was a teacher at a local high school. One day, this freshman named Eduardo came to my friend and asked, "Mister, I want to start a Chess Club will you help me?" My friend Zach didn't know anything about Chess so he enlisted me and my friend Mark's aid.

The first day I met this Eduardo kid, I could tell he was exceptionally bright. But he was a cocky little punk. He bragged about how he won a Chess tournament at school and he was the best player around. And he was the worst trash-talker. I mean, he talked trash the entire game—a Chess game! It was his dream to become a professional Chess player.

On the first day, I played against him and what did he do? He tried to 3-move Checkmate me! He pulled his Queen out first chance he got! Well, I'm no pro, but I know how to shut down a 3-Move checkmate, so I shut it down. But he kept moving his Queen around and I'm sad to say eventually he won.

I'm not gonna lie. He was good at thinking ahead, if only with his Queen.

The next week we played, and he tried it again. By that time, I knew his game. And I knew enough to know that pulling your Queen out early is a bad idea, so I used it against him. I developed my pieces normally and attacked his Queen whenever I could, which forced him to move his precious Queen and lose a turn. Of course, he lost.

At the end of the game, I said, "You know, Eduardo, if you keep your back Queen until you've developed your pieces, you might win more." But of course, he shrugged it off and mumbled, "I win all the time with my Queen."

He kept playing me, and week after week, he kept losing. One day he got so upset he couldn't win that he nearly started crying. Through his shaky voice, he said he wasn't sure if he wanted to play Chess anymore and asked himself out loud how I was beating him when he was a way better player. And I gently reminded the little punk, "If you just keep your Queen back, I promise you'll win more."

The next week, he tried it. He didn't win the first time. His entire strategy was based on a 3-move checkmate, so he didn't know how to develop his pieces normally. So, he asked me, "What am I supposed to do if I don't use   my Queen?"

Aha! This was the defining moment. I showed him how to develop his pieces and convinced him to base his strategy around controlling the center, using forks, castling early, and keeping his Queen back!

The next week he came back with a vengeance. He used the strategies I taught him and he started winning. And winning. And winning. That was the information he needed to soar. After that, I didn't beat Eduardo too often. We found him a new instructor at a higher level and he continues to improve today.

I'm still not sure if I did a good thing helping Eduardo, but the point of the story is if you choose to take your Queen out, your total reign over your friends may be short.

PRINCIPLE #6: WIN THE QUEEN RACE

We've all been there. You're at the end of the game. There are only a few pieces left on the board. You're trying to checkmate your opponent, but you just. Can't. Trap him. His King is running around the board like a chicken with its head cut off, but you can't narrow him down. The end of the game goes for another half hour before you finally just call it a draw.

This part of the game is called the Endgame. As you may or may not know, there are three parts of chess. The Opening, the Middle Game, and the Endgame. It's important to know strategies for all three.

Here, we're going to cover what is, in my opinion, the most important Endgame strategy: **Win the Queen Race.**

The Queen Race starts like this: You're near the end of the game. You probably traded all the way down. You each have a Bishop and a Rook and there are a few Pawns on the board. No one has any immediate means of checkmating the other. What do you do?

Remember Principle #1 when I said to control the center? Forget *that* for the rest of the game! It's time to shift your entire focus to Promoting a Pawn to a Queen!

What!?

That's right. You know how a Pawn is the diddly guy who can't do much except move one space forward and can't even move backward? At the end of the game, that diddly little guy is your HERO because if you move him to your opponent's edge of the board, you can promote him to a Queen!

Remember how we talked about Castling as one of three special moves in chess. Promoting is one of those three special moves and it will save your butt if you prioritize it. Check out this video that will show you what promoting a Pawn to Queen looks like:

What Is Pawn Promotion? | Chess
http://youtu.be/Ulb1UiD4cMY

You can promote to any piece you want (except a Pawn or a King), but 90% of the time, you want to promote to a Queen. It's like one day at work you're a mail clerk and the next day you're the Senior Vice President!

So, how does one go about promoting a Pawn to a Queen? You'll want this Pawn to be the best qualified candidate before you decide to promote him. The following is a list of qualifications you'll want him to have in the order you'd want.

> **First,** find a Pawn that is further ahead than the other Pawns. The ideal candidate is the Pawn that is furthest toward your opponent's edge.

> **Second,** find a Pawn that has no other Pawns or pieces in front of him (in his column).

> **Third,** find a Pawn with protection from a stronger piece. Rooks are great for this. You can also use a Queen, Bishop, or Knight, to protect the square where he will eventually be promoted.

> **Fourth,** find a Pawn that has no enemy pieces in the column next to him. I list this one fourth because this can sometimes work to your advantage.

> **Fifth,** find a Pawn that has a teammate Pawn in the column next to him. That way, if an enemy piece takes him or blocks his path, his Pawn teammate can either protect him or pick up the baton and run for a promotion.

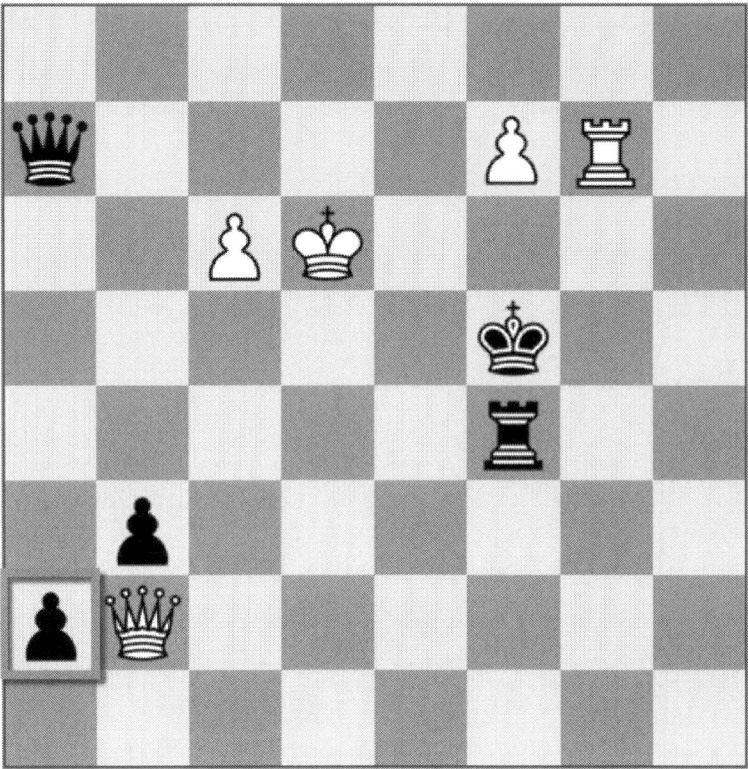

The **picture above** is from an actual game where I was playing as Black. I used the criteria above to determine the Pawn in the red square is the best candidate. It was a close call between this pawn and the pawn slightly ahead of him, but ultimately this one was the better choice because

1. there are no enemy pawns in the column next to it,
2. there are no enemy pawns in front of it
3. the Queen can easily protect the square where my Pawn will be promoted.

Notice that White has equal pieces as me, but White eventually loses because I manage to promote my Pawn to a Queen and White does not have a clear path to promote either of his pawns.

There are probably a hundred different strategies and scenarios you could learn to reinforce this concept. But if you remember one thing, it's this: **do**

everything you can to promote that Pawn!

On the flip side, you also want to do everything you can to prevent your enemy from promoting his or her Pawn. Remember, it's a race. The first person to promote his Pawn to a Queen wins. You *must* **Win the Queen Race. The sooner you shift your focus, the more likely you are to win.** If your enemy gets a Queen before you do, it's off with your King's head!

PRINCIPLE #7: FIGHT FOR A STALEMATE

Speaking of endgame strategy, **Stalemate** is an extremely useful tactic that most novices have heard of, but don't know how to use to their advantage. Hopefully, by following the previous six principles, you won't need this tactic, but if you know you're not going to win, this is your next best bet. Let's start with a definition:

> **Stalemate** is when one player is not in check and cannot move ANY available pieces without putting his or her own King into check.

If you're new to Chess, you may or may not remember that it's illegal to move your own King into check. What a pain! But in this principle, we're going to use that fact to our advantage.

Stalemate occurs most often when one player only has his King and the other player has more powerful pieces. Let's say, for example, that you made some bad choices and you have no pieces left except your King. Your opponent's King, Queen, and Rook are still on the board. Well, your opponent is definitely going to win, right?

Wrong!

An almost empty board is a dangerous place for your opponent because your opponent often won't notice the squares his pieces are covering. Now's the time to **Fight for a Stalemate.**

Before I go on, let me explain *why* you would want your opponent to stalemate you. Many people think that a stalemate is a tie and the person with the most pieces wins. That is incorrect. In most circles, a stalemate means no one wins and you and your opponent don't gain or lose rating points. If you were about to lose, that's pretty good! It's not as good as winning, but it's not as bad as losing!

And let's not forget it deprives your opponent bragging rights. For the aggressor who should have won, a stalemate is embarrassing; if he had been more careful, he could have won and gained all the glory associated with it.

In the **picture below**, the White King is in stalemate. The colored squares represent the coverage by the Black Queen and Rook. Notice that the White's King is not on that coverage but also can't move anywhere.

Since White's King cannot move into check and cannot move onto any of the adjacent squares, and there are no other White pieces on the board, it's a stalemate! The game is over and nobody wins.

In the **video below**, the same dignified man will show you what a stalemate is.

Beginning Chess Lessons: Part 2 : What is a Stalemate in a Chess Game?
https://www.youtube.com/watch?v=4SMfknyjPxc&index=3&list=PL3xEMsX_i6vFPsUh_tSLLt3kAf70IZqea

Here's another example:

Stalemate in chess
https://www.youtube.com/watch?v=cffkAasaZZg&index=4&list=PL3xEMsX_i6vFPsUh_tSLLt3kAf70IZqea

Now that you have a clear idea of what stalemate is. How do you go about it? There are a hundred million ways that a stalemate could occur, but here are a few tips you can use to get your opponent to stalemate you.

1. **Don't give up!** - If there aren't a lot of pieces left in the game, you're more likely to get stalemated. Fight it out to the bitter end.
2. **Sacrifice the Others** - Move your King into a position where he is not checked and can't move anywhere, then sacrifice your other pieces.
   http://www.chess.com/blog/coolthing/how-to-stalemate-yourself
3. **Repetition of Moves** - If the exact same position occurs more than three times, you can claim a stalemate.
4. **50 Moves Rule** - If both sides make 50 moves without moving a Pawn or making a capture, a player can claim a draw.
5. **Draw by agreement** – Ask your opponent if he's ready to call it a draw. If you both agree, time to play again.
6. **Insufficient Mating Material** – See below.

INSUFFICIENT MATING MATERIAL

This advice could save hours of your life. There are certain piece combinations that simply cannot result in a checkmate. Therefore, they must be stalemate. If any of the following combinations occur, you can claim a draw.

1. King vs. King
2. King vs. Bishop and King
3. King vs. Knight and King
4. King vs. Two Knights and King

If you have any of the above combinations, go ahead and call a draw.

ON THE OFFENSIVE

If you're on the offensive side of a potential stalemate, you can do a few things to make sure your opponent doesn't rob you of your glory.

1. **Visualize the squares your pieces are covering**—even your inactive pieces—otherwise you might put him in stalemate without realizing it.
2. **Check the King every time.** If you constantly put him in check, he can't be stalemated.
3. **Give him a way out.** Check that he has an available square to move to before you move. If he has a place to move, he's not going to be stalemated.
4. **Don't kill the (whole) kingdom.** In the end of the game, you might feel compelled to take all his other pieces before you checkmate him. Don't! Leave one non-threatening piece alive. If there's a piece he can move, he can't be stalemated.

Of course, stalemate is largely in the hands of the aggressor. You *will* have to fight for it. But if you're trying to get stalemated and he's not even thinking about it, you have a major advantage.

PRINCIPLE #8: WATCH FOR THE WEAK BACK RANK

Many beginners have an opportunity in front of them they don't see. Watching beginners play, I just want to scream Back Rank! Of course, I don't. But, if I did, it would probably teach them something.

A **Weak Back Rank** occurs frequently in beginner games and it's super easy to exploit if you can recognize it.

This is what you look for. **(See image below)** It's near the end of the game. Most of your opponent's pieces are gone. The opponent's King is on the farthest row. (A row is called a Rank in Chess terms). In front of the Black king, protecting him, are three Pawns. You're playing White. What move would you make?

What move would you make?

Hint: You can checkmate in one move.

In the **image above**, the pawns protecting the Black King are also trapping him! If you know how to recognize this it's the easiest checkmate you'll ever get. All you need to do is find a way to move your Rook to the back rank. **Boom!** Checkmate.

And that's why you **Watch for the Weak Back Rank.** Check out this video illustrating the back rank concept.

Chess Puzzle: Back Rank Mate
https://www.youtube.com/watch?v=2l2TDnXVavc

As you can see from the video, a back rank mate is not always as simple as moving one piece, but recognizing a weak back rank can easily win or lose you the game.

If it's *your* King that's in the back with three pawns in front, you can avoid getting back ranked in a few ways. First and foremost, make sure that you have an escape route. That is, move one of your Pawns up so that your King can duck between a triangle of Pawns to protect himself. Otherwise, make sure you have strong pieces in the back protecting your King.

Of course, there are many variations to the Back Rank. But deftly applying the principle in a game will downright mystify your friends.

There they are, eight principles you can use to conquer your friends. I guarantee that if you learn these and know them well, your Chess game will improve dramatically. You won't have to spend hundreds of dollars getting Chess lessons. You won't have to scour Youtube looking for decent Chess videos. And you won't have to learn complex Chess notation trying to learn it.

While I isolated the eight most critical things you need to know, obviously there's still so much more. If you're an absolute beginner and you've either just learned Chess or only played a few years, your first step is to just play. Play as many games as you can and do post game evaluations.

The biggest part of learning in the early stages of Chess is just getting into the habit of thinking 3 moves ahead, checking that you're not accidentally sacrificing your pieces, protecting your pieces, predicting your opponent's strategy. Those skills mainly come from concentrated practice.

From here, the things you need to know are not so easy. While I'm not an expert, I can direct you toward a few things you need to learn.

1. **Learn an Opening**

There are hundreds of openings out there. Find one White and one Black that appeal to you and learn them. Memorize the first 3 moves so that you can easily play them without thinking. You're also going to want to know different variations on the same opening so that, just in case your opponent throws out something crazy, you can adjust.

At this point you may need to learn some Chess notation, but moving on from here, you're going to need it and...hey, it's not so hard once you sit down and   practice it.

2. Learn a few Mating Patterns

I'm not talking about the mating patterns of the Blue Chested Sparrow on Discovery Channel. I'm talking about common ways that you can Checkmate your opponent. You already know one, the Back Rank Mate.

3. Learn Tactics

This one's harder. There are probably thousands of tactics to learn and the conditions when you will need to use them are harder to recognize, but there are definitely times when I was playing a game and remembered a tactic I learned.

4. Learn more at the theskillartistsguide.com

Of course, I would have loved to cover everything in this book. But my promise to you is to deliver what I think is *the* most important. On my website, I'm going to be posting articles for readers covering a few of the tactics that support the 8 principles in this book. Check it out! And if you like to express yourself through learning new skills, you may enjoy future articles. Get on the list!

CHAPTER 4: TIPS TO ACCELERATE YOUR LEARNING

I've already showed you the principles that will help you improve your Chess game. Here are a few Skill Artist tricks that can help you get better faster.

1. Play Faster

Hands down, my Chess game improved the most when I started playing faster. Originally, I was a very slow Chess player. Now I frequently play 10 minute blitz games.

I discovered when I started playing faster that I actually made *less* mistakes. Having more time did not improve my game, and to this day, more than 10 minutes on my clock does not lead to better choices.

If you're typically a slow player, I would advise playing 40 minute games (20 minutes for each player) to start out. Then, work your way down to 20 minute games. The idea is to play faster than you are comfortable. Pretty soon you'll be comfortable and you'll have to play even faster.

The advantage of playing faster is it forces you to *know* your technique before you move. Having excess time can actually lead to **Decision Fatigue**, which often results in poorer choices later in the game, especially for newer players. Also, the faster you play, the more games you play, and having played more games can give you a better perspective of the middle game and endgame.

On the other hand, I once saw a pair of new players playing very fast. At first, I was impressed...until I saw they were sacrificing their pieces with bloody reckless abandon. So, if you tend to be a fast player, but make a lot of mistakes, try slowing down for a while until you've internalized basic chess and the 8 principles I listed above.

In order to play faster you'll need a Chess Clock. If you play live Chess on Chess.com it automatically clocks your time. Here are a few other free or low-cost choices you can use.

Computer Chess Clock

Here's a Free Chess Clock you can run from an Internet browser:
http://www.online-stopwatch.com/chess-clock/

Chess Clock App for iPhone or Android

These days I would recommend getting an App for your phone. It's the least expensive option and it usually works the best. My favorite Chess Clock App is by Chess.com. It's free and you can find it in the App store. Just go to the app store and search Chess Clock App.

Physical Chess Clock

You can also buy a physical Chess Clock. For some reason, Chess Clocks are heinously expensive. They range from $20 to $70. If it's twenty dollars or less it will probably break within a few months, so I would recommend getting one of the nicer ones. Here are a few suggestions from Amazon:
http://www.amazon.com/s/ref=nb_sb_noss_1?url=search -alias%3Daps&field-keywords=Chess+Clock

2. Strengthen your Chess muscle

Skill artists know that learning a new skill is like strengthening a muscle. **Repeat to Remember**. Here's how you can think of it. If you want stronger biceps, would you go to the gym, do one bicep curl and go home? No! First, you repeat it 9 more times. You do 10 repetitions again. Then again. And *then* you can move on (and hopefully work something other than your bicep, but that's another topic for a Skill Artist's Guide). And a few days later you'll come back to the gym and follow the same routine.

In order to get your brain to remember a skill long term, you must expose it to the new skill consistently for an extended period of time. For example, to learn Chess, I would say practice or play every day for at least a week. Then, you can take a couple days off. But play for another week straight after that. Continue this schedule until you've reached your goal.

Your sessions can be anywhere from 10 minutes to 3 hours. I don't recommend playing more than three hours because your brain fatigues after a while and training stops being effective. Now, if you have to take an extra day off here or there, that's okay. Everybody's schedule is different. But don't take more than a few days off because your Chess muscle will atrophy.

3. Get a Partner or Join a Community

Because humans are naturally social, the brain engages easier when there's a physical person in front of it. Find someone who is at your level or teach him a few of the principles (maybe not all of them, mwahaha) and engage him in friendly competition. After every game, I would encourage you to do a post game analysis. Discuss with your partner why you either lost or won the game. Learn from it and play again.

If you don't have a Chess partner, or even if you do, it's always good to join a community of Chess players. In most cities there are local Chess clubs, just search Google for Chess clubs in your area.

4. Join an Online Community

You can also join an online community. My biggest leaps in Chess came when I joined Chess.com. I highly recommend this site to anyone. You can join for free and play live Chess against people from all over the world. This is a great way to practice your Chess skills. They also have a program called Chess Mentor that teaches you strategy and tactics with a premium membership ($14 a month).

One of the biggest advantages of playing online is you can **Measure your Progress** by getting a rating. It's easy to think you're getting better when...actually you're not. (Trust me I'm guilty of this too.) That's why it's important to find an objective way to measure your progress so you can constantly strive for a better rating and playing online is a great way to do that.

I mentioned Chess.com has a great Chess Clock App. They also have a great general Chess App. You can play live online, learn tactics, and watch Chess videos. I also recommend the Chess with Friends app, which allows you to connect and play with your friends over the internet.

Most people have a Chess program on their computer. I don't recommend playing against a computer to learn Chess because computers don't make the mistakes humans do. You want to play against someone who is at your level and Chess computers either totally destroy you, or they make weird mistakes that don't make sense.

CONCLUSION

I can honestly say some of the best times of my life were playing Chess with my friends and family. I created this book because I wanted to help other casual Chess players engage themselves in this game and I hope that I've helped you accomplish that.

Don't stop here! Good skill artists **Find Multiple Sources**. I've included more Chess books and resources in the Resources section at the end of the book. You can also visit my website at theskillartistsguide.com. Stay in touch and subscribe because I'll be posting other Chess tactics.

While I encourage and love self-education, you can also hire a Chess tutor or join a Chess class. Skill Artists know how and when to get advice. Search google for educators in your area.

Also, **spread the word!** Comments about your experience with the book are very helpful. Share your story with us at the Skill Artist website, my facebook page, amazon.com, maxen@theskillartistsguide.com, or any other place this book is sold.

You might have a significant edge after reading this book, but hey, there's no reason you can't share these secrets. Now is your chance to take what you've learned and give back to the community. Challenge your friends to improve, encourage learning and progress, coach a Chess club, or teach a younger sibling how to play Chess.

Or, completely conquer your friends. Who's keeping tabs?

RESOURCES

Chess for Beginners: A Picture Guide Including Photographs and Diagrams for Self-Teaching

Bobby Fischer Teaches Chess

Chess for Dummies

WEBSITES

Chess.com

Free website where you can play live against people around the world. If you want to improve your Chess game. I recommend a premium membership for $14/month. They have a program called Chess mentor that teaches you everything from how to move the pieces to the most advanced moves.

www.chess.com

Chesscademy

Cool and free website that teaches you the basics through interactive Chess lessons. All the training is free.

www.chesscademy.com

Velocity Chess

New website where you can play for free or win gift cards by wagering.

www.velocitychess.com

Chess with Friends

An app for Android or Iphone where you can play against your friends.

Printed in Great Britain
by Amazon